Christmas Crisis Solutions

Christmas Crisis Solutions

Matthew Petchinsky

Christmas Crisis Solutions: The Ultimate Last-Minute Survival Guide

By: Matthew Petchinsky

Introduction: The Calm Before the Christmas Storm

The twinkling lights are strung, the snow is falling gently, and the holiday spirit is alive—at least, in theory. In reality, the holidays can often feel more like a frantic dash than a serene stroll. We've all been there: the clock is ticking, stores are closing, plans are unraveling, and the magical image of a picture-perfect Christmas seems to slip further out of reach with every passing moment. If you're reading this, you might already feel the weight of last-minute holiday chaos. Take a deep breath—this guide is here to remind you that no matter how close the clock strikes to Christmas, the season can still be saved.

The Holiday Pressure Cooker

Why is it that a season meant for joy and togetherness often brings stress and panic? The holidays come with a unique blend of expectations: the perfect gifts, a dazzlingly decorated home, a table full of delicious food, and enough time to enjoy it all with friends and family. But life doesn't always go as planned. Work runs late, unexpected guests show up, or the one gift you promised to deliver is out of stock everywhere. Add to that the pressure of social media perfection, and it's no wonder the season sometimes feels overwhelming.

Here's the truth: Christmas doesn't have to be perfect to be memorable. In fact, some of the most cherished holiday memories come from those unexpected, imperfect moments. What matters most is creating an atmosphere of warmth, joy, and togetherness—and this guide will help you do just that, even when time and resources are limited.

A New Perspective on Last-Minute Crises

Before diving into the practical solutions, let's take a moment to shift your mindset. Think of last-minute holiday challenges as opportunities to unleash your creativity and resourcefulness. Each problem—whether it's a missing gift, an unexpected guest, or a decorating mishap—has a solution that can spark joy and even create new traditions. The key is staying calm and flexible, approaching each challenge with a sense of humor and a determination to make the best of it.

This book is your secret weapon to navigating the holiday storm with confidence. It's not about aiming for perfection; it's about finding clever, practical ways to keep the Christmas spirit alive no matter the situation. You'll discover that with a little ingenuity and preparation, you can transform any crisis into a festive success.

What You'll Find in This Guide

This book is organized to address the most common holiday hurdles, offering actionable advice that you can implement immediately. Each chapter focuses on a specific challenge, from last-minute gift ideas to quick decorating hacks, and provides step-by-step solutions to help you conquer the chaos. Here's a sneak peek:

- **Need a gift in minutes?** Learn how to craft heartfelt DIY presents or choose digital options that deliver instant joy.
- **No time to cook?** Discover fast, delicious recipes and alternative dining options that save the day.
- **Surprise visitors?** Get tips on hosting guests with ease, even if they show up unannounced.
- **Tech trouble?** Solve common tech issues quickly so your holiday playlist and shopping apps keep running smoothly.

At the end of the book, you'll also find tips for avoiding holiday stress in the future, helping you plan ahead for a smoother and more enjoyable Christmas next year.

Staying Calm Under Pressure

The first and most important step in any crisis is to stay calm. Panicking only makes the situation worse and clouds your ability to think clearly. Remember, the essence of Christmas isn't in the perfectly wrapped presents or the flawless dinner—it's in the laughter, connection, and love shared with those around you. When you feel the pressure mounting, take a moment to pause and breathe deeply. Remind yourself that every problem has a solution, and this guide is here to help you find it.

Here are a few quick tips to keep your cool in the holiday storm:

1. **Prioritize:** Not everything needs to be done immediately. Focus on the tasks that matter most.
2. **Delegate:** Involve family and friends in the preparations—it's a great way to lighten the load and create bonding moments.
3. **Laugh it off:** Humor can turn even the most chaotic moments into fond memories.
4. **Remember your why:** The true meaning of the holidays isn't in the material things; it's in the joy of giving, the comfort of tradition, and the warmth of togetherness.

Let's Save Christmas Together

With this guide in hand, you're equipped to face any holiday crisis with confidence and creativity. Whether you're scrambling for last-minute solutions or just looking for ways to streamline your celebrations, you'll find everything you need to keep the Christmas spirit alive. Remember: even when things don't go as planned, it's the effort, love, and laughter that make the season special.

So, take a deep breath, turn the page, and let's tackle this Christmas storm together. You've got this!

Chapter 1: Holiday Hustle Hacks
Time-Saving Tips to Beat the Clock

The holiday season waits for no one. As the countdown to Christmas begins, time feels like it's slipping away faster than ever. With so much to do and so little time, the key to managing last-minute holiday crunches lies in strategic planning, prioritization, and leveraging modern tools. This chapter will equip you with practical hacks to streamline your efforts and stay on top of your holiday to-do list without losing your mind.

The Power of Prioritization

The first step to beating the holiday clock is identifying what truly matters. Not every task carries the same weight, and trying to do everything at once can lead to burnout. Use these strategies to prioritize effectively:

1. **Divide and Conquer:** Break your to-do list into categories: Must-Do, Nice-to-Do, and Can-Wait. Focus your energy on the Must-Do tasks first, like buying gifts for immediate family or preparing food for holiday gatherings.
2. **Set Non-Negotiables:** Identify two or three tasks that are absolutely essential for your holiday success. For example, securing a tree, buying a key gift, or organizing travel plans.
3. **Time vs. Importance:** Evaluate tasks based on how much time they'll take versus how important they are. Tackle high-impact, low-time tasks first to build momentum.
4. **Delegate Wisely:** Don't be afraid to assign tasks to others. Kids can help with wrapping, partners can pick up groceries, and friends can pitch in with decorating.

Create a Rapid Action Plan

When time is short, planning becomes even more critical. A Rapid Action Plan helps you focus on what needs to happen immediately and ensures no time is wasted. Here's how to create one:

1. **Write It Down:** Start with a brain dump of everything you think you need to do. Then, categorize and prioritize as outlined above.
2. **Set Time Blocks:** Assign specific time frames to each task. For example, dedicate 30 minutes to gift wrapping, one hour for shopping, and 15 minutes for cleaning a key room.
3. **Use Deadlines:** Set mini-deadlines for yourself. If shopping needs to be done by noon, stick to that timeline.
4. **Stay Flexible:** Be prepared to adapt if something takes longer than expected or an unexpected task arises. Leave a little buffer time between tasks.

Leverage Technology to Save Time

Modern technology offers countless tools to make holiday preparations more efficient. Here are some of the best apps and digital hacks:

1. **Task Management Apps:** Use apps like **Trello**, **Asana**, or **Todoist** to organize your tasks and keep track of deadlines.
2. **Grocery Delivery Services:** Save hours by using apps like **Instacart**, **Shipt**, or store-specific options for grocery delivery or curbside pickup.
3. **Gift-Finding Tools:** Turn to platforms like **Giftster** or **Elfster** to create gift lists, share them with family, and avoid duplications.
4. **Shopping Shortcuts:** Apps like **Honey** and **Rakuten** can find discounts automatically, saving you time and money while shopping online.
5. **Smart Reminders:** Use voice assistants like Alexa, Siri, or Google Assistant to set reminders for tasks throughout the day.

6. **Delivery Trackers:** Apps like **Shop** consolidate all your delivery tracking in one place, so you don't have to search through emails.

Efficiency Tips for Common Holiday Tasks

Sometimes, simple tweaks to everyday tasks can save hours. Here are specific time-saving hacks for common holiday activities:

1. **Gift Wrapping:**
   - Use pre-decorated gift bags or reusable fabric wraps for ultra-fast wrapping.
   - Wrap gifts assembly-line style: lay out all supplies, wrap one type of gift at a time, and work in batches.
   - Skip the bows and ribbons if you're short on time; a well-folded wrap with a gift tag works just as well.

2. **Decorating:**
   - Focus on high-impact areas like the living room, dining table, or front porch instead of decorating the whole house.
   - Use pre-lit garlands, plug-in window candles, or LED light projectors for quick yet festive results.
   - Repurpose existing decorations for multiple uses. For example, ornaments can double as table centerpieces.

3. **Meal Prep:**
   - Plan meals that use overlapping ingredients to cut down on prep time. For example, a roasted chicken can become sandwiches, salads, or soup.
   - Take advantage of store-bought shortcuts like pre-chopped vegetables, pre-baked desserts, or frozen side dishes.
   - Use one-pot or sheet pan recipes to save on cleanup time.

Mindset Hacks for Staying Productive

Time management isn't just about external tools and strategies; your mindset plays a huge role in staying focused and productive under pressure. Here are a few mental shifts to keep you on track:

1. **Embrace Imperfection:** Not everything needs to be Instagram-worthy. Focus on creating joyful memories rather than achieving picture-perfect results.
2. **Stay Present:** Avoid multitasking when it's counterproductive. Concentrate fully on one task at a time to finish it more quickly and efficiently.
3. **Celebrate Small Wins:** Checking off even one small task can provide a sense of accomplishment and motivation to keep going.

When the Clock Runs Out

Sometimes, even the best-laid plans can fall short. If you find yourself truly out of time, here's how to pivot gracefully:

1. **Shift the Focus:** If you can't complete a task (e.g., perfect decorations), shift the focus to what matters most: spending time with loved ones.
2. **Go Digital:** When physical gifts aren't an option, consider sending e-gift cards, digital subscriptions, or online experiences.
3. **Simplify:** Instead of an elaborate meal, focus on a few key dishes or even order takeout.
4. **Turn to Tradition:** When all else fails, lean into meaningful traditions like storytelling, singing carols, or sharing gratitude around the table.

Conclusion

Holiday hustle doesn't have to mean holiday stress. By prioritizing effectively, leveraging technology, and using these time-saving tips, you can make the most of every minute. Remember, it's not about doing everything; it's about doing what matters most. With your Rapid Action Plan in place, you're ready to tackle the rest of this guide and sail through the holiday season with confidence.

Chapter 2: Emergency Gift Solutions
No Gift? No Problem!

The sinking realization that you've forgotten a gift—or simply run out of time to buy one—can be a stressful holiday moment. But Christmas isn't about the cost of the gift; it's about the thought behind it. Whether the stores are closed, inventory is depleted, or you're just crunched for time, this chapter is packed with creative, thoughtful, and quick solutions to ensure you can give something meaningful.

The Last-Minute Gift Mindset

Before diving into specific solutions, it's important to embrace a mindset of creativity and resourcefulness. The key to a great last-minute gift isn't perfection—it's showing the recipient that you care. Thoughtfulness trumps price tags every time, and a simple, well-executed idea can leave a lasting impression.

Keep these principles in mind:

1. **Personalization:** A personal touch elevates even the simplest gift.
2. **Utility:** Practical gifts are always appreciated.
3. **Presentation:** A little effort in how you present the gift can make a big difference.

DIY Gifts That Delight

Handmade gifts are perfect for last-minute situations because they can be created using items you already have at home. Here are some quick and easy DIY ideas:

1. **Mason Jar Mixes:** Layer dry ingredients for cookies, brownies, or hot cocoa in a mason jar. Add a handwritten recipe card and tie with a ribbon for a cozy, personal touch.
2. **Customized Candles:** Use plain candles and decorate them with ribbons, charms, or pressed flowers. You can also personalize them with a scent by rubbing essential oils into the wax.
3. **Memory Jars:** Write down favorite memories or affirmations on small pieces of paper and place them in a jar. Add a note encouraging the recipient to pull one out whenever they need a smile.
4. **Handwritten Coupons:** Create a booklet of coupons for meaningful gestures, like "One Free Movie Night," "Breakfast in Bed," or "An Evening of Babysitting."
5. **Photo Gifts:** Print a favorite photo and frame it. If you're out of frames, create a DIY stand using cardboard or clothespins.
6. **Homemade Treats:** Bake cookies, make chocolate-dipped pretzels, or create a festive trail mix. Package them in decorative bags or tins for a polished look.
7. **Crafty Keychains or Jewelry:** Use beads, charms, and other materials you have at home to create simple but heartfelt accessories.

Digital Gifts for Instant Delivery

When time is of the essence, digital gifts are a lifesaver. They're instant, thoughtful, and often customizable. Here are some popular options:

1. **Streaming Subscriptions:** Give the gift of entertainment with a subscription to Netflix, Hulu, Disney+, or Spotify.
2. **E-Books or Audiobooks:** Services like Kindle or Audible allow you to gift a specific book or a membership.
3. **Online Courses:** For the learner in your life, gift a course on platforms like Udemy, MasterClass, or Skillshare.
4. **Virtual Experiences:** Purchase tickets for virtual tours, cooking classes, or fitness sessions.
5. **Gift Cards:** Digital gift cards for Amazon, iTunes, or local restaurants are always a hit. Add a note suggesting what they could use it for to make it more personal.
6. **Personalized Videos:** Use platforms like Cameo to have a favorite celebrity or influencer record a message for your recipient.
7. **Donations in Their Name:** For the altruistic recipient, make a donation to a cause they care about and share the details in a heartfelt card.

Experience-Based Gifts

Giving experiences instead of physical items can be a memorable and meaningful alternative, even at the last minute:

1. **Tickets to Local Events:** Purchase tickets to a concert, play, or sports game they'd love. Print or email the confirmation.
2. **DIY "Experience Vouchers":** Write up a voucher for a planned outing, like a day at the museum, a hike with a picnic, or a home-cooked dinner party.
3. **Memberships or Subscriptions:** Consider memberships to local attractions like zoos, botanical gardens, or gyms.
4. **At-Home Spa Day:** Gather items like face masks, lotions, and candles (or purchase a spa kit online for quick delivery) and create a relaxing experience.
5. **Cooking Class Night:** Purchase the ingredients for a specific recipe and offer to cook it together for a fun bonding experience.

Gifts You Can Source Locally

Even when stores are closing or the shelves are empty, you can still find excellent gifts locally if you know where to look:

1. **Grocery Stores:** Look for gourmet items like specialty chocolates, wine, cheese, or coffee. Create a mini gift basket by combining a few items.
2. **Pharmacies:** Pharmacies often stock beauty kits, candles, and small gadgets that make great gifts in a pinch.
3. **Local Bakeries or Cafés:** Pick up a box of festive cookies, pastries, or a gift card.
4. **Gas Stations:** Believe it or not, some gas stations have great small gifts like quirky mugs, local products, or even prepaid gift cards.
5. **Farmers' Markets:** Handcrafted soaps, candles, jams, or artisanal products can make unique and thoughtful gifts.

Presentation: The Finishing Touch

No matter how simple the gift, thoughtful presentation can elevate it to something extraordinary. If you're out of traditional wrapping materials, try these alternatives:

1. **Reusable Bags:** Use a pretty tote bag or a drawstring pouch that doubles as part of the gift.
2. **Fabric Wrap:** Wrap gifts in festive fabric, scarves, or even a cozy blanket.
3. **Newspaper or Magazines:** Use colorful pages or comic strips for a creative, eco-friendly wrap.
4. **Decorative Boxes:** Repurpose any decorative box you have at home. Add a bow for a finishing touch.
5. **Nature's Decorations:** Use pinecones, sprigs of evergreen, or dried orange slices as embellishments for a rustic look.

Emergency Group Gifting

If you're part of a group and everyone is scrambling for a gift, consider pooling resources for a joint present:

1. **Crowdfunded Gift Cards:** Everyone chips in for a larger gift card to their favorite store.
2. **Group Experience:** Organize a group outing or cover tickets for a shared activity.
3. **Big-Ticket Item:** Combine funds for a high-value item, like a piece of tech or a luxury item they wouldn't purchase themselves.

Conclusion: Gifts from the Heart

At its core, gift-giving is about showing appreciation and love—not about the price tag or presentation. Whether it's a heartfelt DIY creation, a thoughtfully chosen digital gift, or a quick pick from the grocery store, your effort and intention are what truly matter. With these emergency solutions, you can face any last-minute gifting challenge with

confidence and creativity, ensuring that your holiday season is full of smiles and gratitude.

Chapter 3: Grocery Store Scramble
Finding Festive Feasts on a Deadline

Picture this: it's Christmas Eve, and your kitchen is missing crucial ingredients for the big holiday meal. You dash to the grocery store, only to find picked-over shelves and crowds of equally stressed shoppers. If this scenario sounds familiar, don't worry—you're not alone. This chapter will teach you how to navigate grocery stores during the holiday rush, make smart substitutions, and whip up delicious meals even when supplies are scarce and time is limited.

The Last-Minute Grocery Store Game Plan

Approaching the grocery store without a plan can lead to wasted time, unnecessary purchases, and even more stress. Before you set foot in the store, take these steps to streamline your trip:

1. **Make a List (and Stick to It):** Write down exactly what you need to avoid aimless wandering and impulse buys. Organize your list by store sections (e.g., produce, dairy, pantry) for faster navigation.
2. **Prioritize Essentials:** Identify the must-have items for your meal and focus on those first. If substitutions are needed, tackle them in real time.
3. **Shop Off-Hours:** If possible, avoid peak shopping times (late afternoon or early evening) to minimize crowds and long lines. Early mornings are usually quieter.
4. **Use Technology:** Check store apps or websites to see what's in stock or order online for curbside pickup if time allows.
5. **Bring a Backup Plan:** Have a list of substitutions or alternative recipes ready in case key ingredients are unavailable.

Must-Have Items for Festive Feasts

If you're racing through the store, focus on these versatile staples to build a holiday-worthy meal:

1. **Proteins:**
   - Main dishes like chicken, turkey, ham, or beef are classic, but if these are out of stock, consider alternatives like pork loin, salmon, or rotisserie chicken.
   - Vegetarian options: Tofu, tempeh, or a hearty bean dish can work as a centerpiece.

2. **Starches:**
   - Stock up on potatoes (mashed, roasted, or baked), pasta, rice, or bread.
   - Frozen alternatives like pre-made mashed potatoes or garlic bread can save time.

3. **Vegetables:**
   - Focus on what's fresh and available. Carrots, green beans, Brussels sprouts, and spinach are versatile options.
   - Grab frozen vegetables as backups—they're quick to cook and retain nutrients.

4. **Dairy and Eggs:**
   - Butter, cream, and cheese are staples for sauces, side dishes, and desserts. If cream is out of stock, half-and-half or even whole milk can work in a pinch.
   - Eggs are essential for baking, binding, and breakfast dishes.

5. **Pantry Staples:**
   - Stock up on canned goods like beans, broth, and tomato products.
   - Spices, olive oil, flour, sugar, and baking powder are essential for cooking and baking.

6. **Dessert Basics:**
   - Pre-made pie crusts, boxed cake mixes, and frozen desserts are lifesavers when time is short.

- Pick up holiday cookies or chocolates if baking isn't an option.
7. **Drinks:**
   - Don't forget beverages! Grab wine, cider, sparkling water, or ingredients for hot cocoa.

Smart Substitutions for Scarce Ingredients

If shelves are empty, don't panic—many ingredients can be substituted with what's available. Here are some common swaps:

- **Milk:** Use evaporated milk, powdered milk, or plant-based milk (unsweetened varieties).
- **Butter:** Replace with margarine, shortening, or even oil (use ¾ cup oil for 1 cup butter).
- **Cream:** Mix ¾ cup milk with ¼ cup melted butter for 1 cup of heavy cream.
- **Eggs:** For baking, use ¼ cup applesauce, mashed banana, or yogurt per egg. Flaxseed mixed with water (1 tbsp flaxseed + 3 tbsp water) also works.
- **Flour:** Substitute with gluten-free flour blends, almond flour, or even finely ground oats.
- **Meat:** Swap one protein for another (e.g., turkey for chicken) or use plant-based proteins like lentils or mushrooms.
- **Sugar:** Replace white sugar with brown sugar, honey, or maple syrup (adjust liquid content accordingly).

Quick and Easy Recipes for Festive Feasts

When time is tight, simple recipes can still deliver big holiday flavors. Here are a few ideas:

Main Course:

Sheet Pan Herb Chicken and Vegetables

- Ingredients: Chicken thighs or drumsticks, potatoes, carrots, onions, olive oil, and seasoning.
- Method: Toss everything on a sheet pan with oil and spices, roast at 400°F for 30–40 minutes.

Holiday Pasta Bake

- Ingredients: Pasta, marinara sauce, ricotta cheese, shredded mozzarella, and any protein (ground turkey, sausage, or tofu).
- Method: Layer cooked pasta with sauce, cheese, and protein in a baking dish. Bake at 375°F for 25–30 minutes.

Side Dishes:

Garlic Mashed Potatoes

- Ingredients: Potatoes, garlic, butter, and milk (or cream).
- Method: Boil and mash potatoes, sauté garlic in butter, and mix together with milk.

Honey-Glazed Carrots

- Ingredients: Carrots, butter, honey, and salt.
- Method: Sauté carrots in butter, drizzle with honey, and cook until tender.

Desserts:
No-Bake Chocolate Truffles

- Ingredients: Chocolate, cream, and cocoa powder.
- Method: Melt chocolate with cream, chill, and roll into balls. Coat with cocoa powder or sprinkles.

Instant Holiday Cheesecake Cups

- Ingredients: Cream cheese, sugar, graham crackers, and canned pie filling.
- Method: Mix cream cheese with sugar, layer with crushed graham crackers and pie filling in cups.

Stress-Free Checkout Strategies
To avoid added frustration during your trip, keep these tips in mind:

1. **Use Self-Checkout:** If your store offers self-checkout, it can save time, especially with smaller purchases.
2. **Check for Express Lanes:** Look for express lanes with fewer items to expedite your trip.
3. **Skip the Cart:** If you're only grabbing a few items, use a basket for easier mobility through crowded aisles.
4. **Pack Smart:** Keep reusable bags handy for quick packing and unloading.

Beyond the Grocery Store: Alternative Sources

If your local store is out of essentials, think creatively about where to shop:

- **Farmers' Markets:** Great for fresh produce, local dairy, and artisanal products.
- **Convenience Stores:** Surprisingly good for staples like eggs, milk, and snacks.
- **Online Delivery Services:** Use apps like Instacart or Amazon Fresh for same-day delivery or pickup.
- **Specialty Stores:** Visit bakeries, butcher shops, or ethnic markets for unique options.

Conclusion: Feasts Without the Frustration

A last-minute grocery store scramble doesn't have to derail your holiday plans. With a focused plan, creative substitutions, and simple recipes, you can transform even the most chaotic shopping trip into a holiday success. Remember, it's not the complexity of the meal that matters—it's the love and effort you put into bringing people together around the table. Now, grab your list and get ready to turn your scramble into a celebration!

Chapter 4: Alternative Dining Options
When the Kitchen Closes (or Burns)

Sometimes, even the best-laid holiday plans go awry. Maybe the turkey didn't thaw in time, the oven gave out, or an enthusiastic attempt at a new recipe turned into a culinary disaster. Or perhaps you simply ran out of time to cook. Whatever the reason, you still have options to save the day and enjoy a festive meal. This chapter provides a wealth of solutions, from quick takeout ideas to hidden gem restaurants and clever meal hacks that require minimal effort.

Why Alternative Dining Options Work

The holidays are about connection, not perfection. Whether you're ordering takeout, dining out, or improvising with what you have, the goal is to share a meal with loved ones. Embracing alternative dining doesn't mean you're giving up—it means you're resourceful. These options can be just as memorable and enjoyable as a traditional home-cooked feast.

Takeout to the Rescue

Takeout is a lifesaver when the kitchen is out of commission or when time is running short. Here's how to make the most of this option:

1. **Plan Ahead if Possible:** Many restaurants take pre-orders for holiday meals. Even if it's Christmas Day, call ahead to confirm availability and avoid long waits.
2. **Go Family-Style:** Choose dishes that serve multiple people, like trays of pasta, platters of chicken, or large pizzas, to make sharing easy.
3. **Consider Specialty Restaurants:** Chinese, Indian, and Mediterranean restaurants are often open on Christmas Day and can provide a unique twist to your holiday meal.

4. **Mix and Match:** Order appetizers from one restaurant, mains from another, and dessert from a third to create a diverse, exciting spread.
5. **Keep It Simple:** Opt for dishes that don't require reheating or assembly, such as sandwiches, sushi, or salads.

Meal Delivery Apps

In today's digital world, meal delivery apps can save the day when you're in a pinch. Popular options include:

1. **Uber Eats, DoorDash, Grubhub, and Postmates:** These apps connect you with local restaurants and allow you to order everything from fast food to gourmet meals.
2. **Grocery Delivery with Pre-Made Options:** Services like Instacart, Walmart+, or Amazon Fresh often include pre-made holiday meals or rotisserie chickens that can be delivered within hours.
3. **Specialty Services:** Apps like Goldbelly ship specialty foods from famous restaurants across the country, perfect for adding a gourmet touch to your holiday table.
4. **Subscription Kits:** If you're planning ahead, meal kits like HelloFresh or Blue Apron can provide pre-measured ingredients for a quick, no-fail holiday meal.

Hidden Gem Restaurants Open on Christmas Day

While many establishments close for the holiday, some remain open and ready to serve. Here's how to find them:

1. **Check Local Listings:** Use Google Maps, Yelp, or OpenTable to search for restaurants open on Christmas Day. Many establishments update their hours online.
2. **Hotels:** Hotel restaurants often remain open during the holidays and may offer special Christmas menus. These can range from buffet-style feasts to upscale dining experiences.
3. **Ethnic Restaurants:** Many Chinese, Indian, and Middle Eastern restaurants stay open on Christmas, offering delicious alternatives to traditional holiday fare.
4. **Diners and 24/7 Spots:** Classic diners and 24-hour chains like Denny's or IHOP often keep their doors open during the holidays, making them reliable options for a warm meal.
5. **Local Community Centers or Churches:** Some organizations host community holiday dinners, which can be a wonderful way to share a meal and connect with others.

Convenience Store and Deli Hacks

If dining out or ordering in isn't an option, turn to your local convenience store or deli for a quick fix. Here's what to look for:

1. **Ready-to-Eat Meals:** Many stores offer rotisserie chickens, premade sandwiches, and microwavable meals.
2. **Snacks as Sides:** Chips, crackers, and hummus can double as appetizers or sides in a pinch.
3. **Frozen Entrees:** Lasagna, pizzas, or pot pies can be baked quickly for a hearty meal.
4. **Dessert Fixes:** Ice cream, cookies, or even a store-bought pie can round out the meal.

5. **Beverages:** Don't forget to grab wine, cider, or sparkling water to add a festive touch.

Emergency Home-Cooking Hacks

If you're determined to stay home but the kitchen isn't fully functional, here are some no-cook or minimal-cook ideas:

1. **Charcuterie Boards:** Assemble a mix of cheeses, cured meats, crackers, fruits, and nuts for an elegant yet effortless centerpiece.
2. **Soup and Sandwich Combos:** Heat canned soup and pair it with deli sandwiches or grilled cheese.
3. **Instant Pot Magic:** Use an Instant Pot or slow cooker to quickly prepare soups, stews, or even a small roast with minimal effort.
4. **Microwave-Friendly Meals:** Many side dishes, like mashed potatoes, rice, or steamed vegetables, can be prepared in the microwave in minutes.
5. **Salad Bar at Home:** Use pre-washed greens and toppings like shredded cheese, croutons, and nuts to create a fresh and easy side dish.

Turning Alternative Dining into a Festive Experience

Even if your holiday meal comes from a restaurant or convenience store, you can make it feel special with a few thoughtful touches:

1. **Set the Table:** Use your best dishes, candles, and holiday decorations to create a festive atmosphere.
2. **Personalize the Menu:** Give fun names to each dish (e.g., "Santa's Special Stir-Fry" or "Jingle Bell Burgers") to add a holiday twist.
3. **Play Holiday Music:** Background music can set the tone and create a warm, festive ambiance.
4. **Serve Family-Style:** Place all the dishes on the table and let everyone help themselves for a communal, celebratory vibe.

5. **Add a Toast:** Begin the meal with a heartfelt toast to the season, acknowledging everyone's presence and the joy of being together.

The Gift of Letting Go

Sometimes, the best way to salvage a difficult holiday meal situation is to embrace the imperfection. Maybe you're eating pizza instead of turkey or enjoying Chinese takeout instead of a traditional feast—but what truly matters is the company, not the cuisine. The unexpected can create cherished memories, from laughing over burnt side dishes to discovering a new favorite restaurant tradition.

Conclusion: A Feast, No Matter the Circumstances

When the kitchen closes—or burns—you don't have to sacrifice a memorable holiday meal. Whether you're relying on takeout, delivery, dining out, or cobbling together a meal from convenience store finds, you can still create a joyful and delicious experience. The holidays are about the moments you share, not the perfection of the meal. So take a deep breath, get creative, and enjoy the feast—whatever it may look like!

Chapter 5: Wrapping Woes
Creative Wrapping Without Wrapping Paper

Wrapping gifts is an art that elevates even the simplest present into something magical. But what happens when you run out of wrapping paper at the last minute? Don't panic—your home is likely filled with creative, sustainable, and even more charming alternatives. This chapter explores innovative ways to wrap gifts using non-traditional materials, showing you how to craft memorable packaging that's both resourceful and visually appealing.

The Beauty of Non-Traditional Wrapping

Before diving into specific materials, let's appreciate the advantages of thinking outside the (gift) box:

1. **Sustainability:** Using repurposed or reusable materials reduces waste, making your wrapping eco-friendly.
2. **Creativity:** Non-traditional wrapping allows for unique and personalized designs that stand out under the tree.
3. **Convenience:** Many of these materials are already in your home, saving you a trip to the store during the holiday rush.
4. **Budget-Friendly:** Save money by repurposing everyday items instead of buying expensive wrapping paper and accessories.

Alternative Wrapping Materials

Here are some creative, practical, and stylish alternatives to traditional wrapping paper:

1. Newspaper and Magazines

- **Why It Works:** Newspapers and magazines offer bold prints, headlines, and imagery that can make for eye-catching wraps.
- **How to Use:** Choose colorful pages, comics, or even crossword sections. Wrap as you would with traditional paper and secure with tape or twine.
- **Enhancements:** Add a ribbon, a sprig of greenery, or a handwritten tag for a polished look.

2. Fabric and Scarves

- **Why It Works:** Fabric wraps are reusable, versatile, and lend an elegant touch to your gifts.
- **How to Use:** Use scarves, tea towels, bandanas, or even pieces of old clothing. Wrap the gift furoshiki-style (a Japanese wrapping technique) by tying the fabric into knots.
- **Enhancements:** Attach a brooch, button, or charm to the knot for added flair.

3. Reusable Bags

- **Why It Works:** A reusable bag doubles as both wrapping and a functional part of the gift.
- **How to Use:** Place the gift inside a tote bag, drawstring pouch, or cloth grocery bag. Tie the handles together or use a festive ribbon to secure.
- **Enhancements:** Choose bags with fun patterns or designs that match the holiday theme.

4. Brown Paper Bags

- **Why It Works:** Simple and rustic, brown paper bags are easy to customize and style.
- **How to Use:** Cut the bag flat and use it as wrapping paper, or place the gift inside and fold or tie the top shut.
- **Enhancements:** Decorate with stamps, drawings, or handwritten messages. Tie with twine or a colorful ribbon for a charming finish.

5. Old Maps and Sheet Music

- **Why It Works:** These materials are unique and offer a touch of nostalgia or sophistication.
- **How to Use:** Wrap gifts as you would with paper. Sheet music is perfect for music lovers, and maps are great for travel enthusiasts.
- **Enhancements:** Use metallic pens to highlight areas on the map or add a personal note about a song on the sheet music.

6. Jars and Containers

- **Why It Works:** Jars, tins, and other containers eliminate the need for wrapping altogether.
- **How to Use:** Fill jars with small gifts, treats, or homemade goodies. For larger gifts, use decorative tins or sturdy boxes.
- **Enhancements:** Tie a bow around the lid or attach a gift tag. Add filler like tissue paper or shredded paper for extra flair.

7. Clothing

- **Why It Works:** Wrapping a gift in a piece of clothing, such as a sweater or blanket, adds a cozy, functional touch.

- **How to Use:** Fold the clothing item around the gift and secure with a ribbon or belt.
- **Enhancements:** Choose festive or winter-themed clothing for a seasonal vibe.

Decorative Accessories

Non-traditional wrapping often benefits from creative finishing touches. Here are some ideas to make your wrapping pop:

1. **Natural Elements:** Use sprigs of pine, holly, rosemary, or cinnamon sticks for a rustic, festive touch.
2. **Handmade Tags:** Cut tags from cardstock, cereal boxes, or leftover cardboard. Personalize with handwritten messages or small drawings.
3. **Twine and Yarn:** Replace ribbon with twine, yarn, or string. Experiment with braiding or layering for added texture.
4. **Buttons and Beads:** Sew or glue buttons and beads onto fabric wraps for a playful, colorful detail.
5. **Stamped Designs:** Use rubber stamps or stencils to add patterns and motifs to plain paper or bags.

Innovative Wrapping Techniques

Get creative with how you present your gifts using these unique techniques:

1. **Layered Wrapping:** Combine materials, like wrapping a gift in brown paper and adding a fabric band around the center.
2. **Pockets and Envelopes:** Create pockets or envelopes out of paper or fabric to hold small items like jewelry or gift cards.
3. **Origami Wraps:** Fold your paper into intricate designs to add a personal and artistic touch.
4. **See-Through Layers:** Use cellophane or translucent fabric over colorful paper for a modern, layered look.

Tips for Wrapping Odd-Shaped Items

Wrapping irregularly shaped gifts can be tricky, but these techniques make it easier:

1. **Gift Bags:** Place the item in a reusable bag or make one using fabric or paper.
2. **Tissue Bundles:** Wrap the gift in tissue paper and secure the top with a ribbon, creating a pouch.
3. **Boxes and Containers:** Place the item in a sturdy box or tin to simplify wrapping.
4. **Shrink Wrap:** Use clear shrink wrap for items like gift baskets. Heat gently with a hairdryer to tighten.

Creating a Wrapping Station at Home

A designated wrapping station can streamline the process, even at the last minute. Include:

- Scissors, tape, and glue
- Ribbons, twine, and yarn
- Markers, pens, and tags
- Wrapping materials like newspaper, fabric, and bags
- Decorative items like greenery, stickers, and stamps

The Joy of Thoughtful Presentation

Even without traditional wrapping paper, you can create a memorable unwrapping experience. Thoughtful presentation turns any gift into something special. Personal touches like handwritten notes, inside jokes, or customized decorations make your wrapping as meaningful as the gift itself.

Conclusion: Wrapping Without the Wrapping Paper

Running out of wrapping paper is no longer a crisis—it's an opportunity to get creative, resourceful, and sustainable. From repurposed newspaper to elegant fabric wraps, the possibilities are endless. Embrace these innovative ideas and make your gifts stand out under the tree. Remember, it's the thought and effort behind the wrapping that truly matters.

Chapter 6: Travel Troubleshooting
Making It Home for the Holidays

The holidays are meant for togetherness, but getting home to loved ones can be a challenge when travel plans hit a snag. From weather-related delays to unexpected car trouble, the holiday season is ripe with potential obstacles. This chapter provides a detailed guide to navigating last-minute travel issues, offering solutions for overcoming weather disruptions, vehicle breakdowns, and finding alternative transportation.

Preparation: Avoiding Last-Minute Disasters

A little preparation can go a long way in minimizing travel stress. Before embarking on your journey, take these steps to set yourself up for success:

1. **Have a Backup Plan:** Familiarize yourself with alternative routes, nearby transportation hubs, and emergency lodging options in case of disruptions.
2. **Pack an Emergency Kit:** Include essentials such as:
   - Phone chargers and backup power banks.
   - Snacks, water, and basic toiletries.
   - A first-aid kit and any necessary medications.
   - Weather-appropriate clothing and blankets.
   - Flashlights, batteries, and a small tool kit if driving.
3. **Check Your Travel Itinerary:** Confirm reservations for flights, buses, trains, or hotels at least 24 hours in advance.
4. **Stay Informed:** Use apps like Waze, Google Maps, or MyRadar to monitor traffic, weather, and delays in real-time.

Dealing with Weather Delays

Inclement weather can derail even the best-laid travel plans. Here's how to stay ahead of weather-related challenges:

1. At the Airport

- **Monitor Flight Status:** Stay updated through your airline's app or websites like FlightAware for live tracking.
- **Act Quickly:** If your flight is delayed or canceled, rebook as soon as possible via the airline app, website, or hotline to secure the best options.
- **Check Nearby Airports:** Alternate airports may have better availability. Consider a short drive to catch a replacement flight.
- **Seek Compensation:** Many airlines provide meal vouchers, hotel stays, or rebooking services during significant delays—check their policies.

2. On the Road

- **Plan Safe Routes:** Use GPS apps to identify roads with less severe weather or alternate routes to bypass closures.
- **Drive Cautiously:** In poor conditions, reduce speed, maintain longer following distances, and avoid sudden braking or acceleration.
- **Carry Emergency Equipment:** Items like snow chains, a small shovel, and kitty litter for traction can be lifesavers in icy conditions.

3. Trains and Buses

- **Stay Updated:** Check with your carrier for real-time updates on delays or cancellations. Many companies offer text or email alerts.

- **Seek Rebooking Options:** Request tickets on the next available departure or explore other carriers that serve the same route.
- **Pack Essentials:** Keep snacks, water, and a blanket handy in case of extended delays.

Overcoming Car Trouble

Road trips are a holiday tradition for many, but car trouble can quickly derail your journey. Here's how to handle common problems:

1. Flat Tires

- **Tools to Carry:** Keep a spare tire, jack, and lug wrench in your car. A portable tire inflator or patch kit can also be useful for temporary fixes.
- **Roadside Assistance:** Memberships like AAA or apps like Urgent.ly can provide tire replacement services if needed.

2. Dead Battery

- **Prepare in Advance:** Carry jumper cables or a portable jump starter in your car.
- **DIY Solution:** If safe, use jumper cables with another car to recharge your battery.

3. Overheating Engine

- **Immediate Action:** Pull over, turn off the engine, and let it cool before opening the hood.

- **Carry Supplies:** Keep extra coolant and water in your car for emergencies.

4. Breakdown in Remote Areas

- **Stay Safe:** Turn on your hazard lights and set up reflective triangles if you have them. Stay in your car unless it's unsafe.
- **Call for Help:** Use roadside assistance services or emergency hotlines. Provide your exact location using GPS coordinates.

Alternate Transportation Options

When your original plans fall apart, alternate transportation can save the day. Here are some options to consider:

1. Ride-Sharing Services

- Apps like Uber and Lyft operate in most urban and suburban areas. For longer trips, inquire about "Uber Hourly" or long-distance rides.

2. Car Rentals

- **Last-Minute Rentals:** Companies like Enterprise, Hertz, and Turo often have cars available for same-day rentals.
- **One-Way Rentals:** If your plans are flexible, consider a one-way rental to your destination.

3. Public Transit

- **Trains and Buses:** Amtrak, Greyhound, and regional bus lines may still have availability for holiday travelers.
- **Local Transit:** Check if metro systems or shuttle services can cover part of your journey.

4. Flights

- Use apps like Skyscanner or Google Flights to find last-minute deals.
- Consider alternative airlines or smaller airports for more availability.

Traveling with Kids or Pets

Traveling with little ones or furry friends adds complexity. Here's how to make it smoother:

1. For Kids

- **Pack Entertainment:** Bring books, games, or tablets with pre-downloaded shows to keep them occupied during delays.
- **Keep Snacks Handy:** Familiar snacks can help avoid meltdowns during long waits.
- **Comfort Items:** A favorite blanket or stuffed toy can make unfamiliar situations feel less stressful.

2. For Pets

- **Pet-Friendly Stops:** Use apps like BringFido to locate pet-friendly hotels and rest stops.
- **Essentials Bag:** Pack food, water, bowls, a leash, and any necessary medications.
- **Car Safety:** Secure pets with a travel crate or harness for their safety.

Overnight Stays and Layovers

Sometimes, delays mean an unexpected overnight stay. Here's how to make the best of it:

1. **Find Nearby Accommodations:** Apps like HotelTonight can help you locate last-minute lodging.
2. **Ask for Discounts:** Many hotels near airports offer reduced rates for stranded travelers.
3. **Stay Comfortable:** Pack a travel pillow, blanket, and toiletries to make a layover more bearable if you can't leave the station or airport.

Mindset: Staying Calm Under Pressure

Unexpected travel issues can be frustrating, but keeping a positive mindset makes a big difference. Here's how to stay composed:

1. **Focus on Solutions:** Concentrate on what you can control, such as rebooking or finding alternative routes.
2. **Stay Flexible:** Be open to changing plans and trying new options, even if they're not what you originally envisioned.
3. **Take Breaks:** If you feel overwhelmed, pause for a moment to regroup and recharge before moving forward.
4. **Communicate:** Keep loved ones updated about delays and revised plans to alleviate concerns.

Conclusion: Making It Home, No Matter What

Holiday travel may come with its fair share of challenges, but with preparation, adaptability, and the right tools, you can overcome any obstacle. Whether it's finding an alternate route, rebooking a flight, or navigating car trouble, the ultimate goal is to arrive safely and enjoy the time with your loved ones. Remember, the journey is part of the adventure—and sometimes, the unexpected detours create the most memorable stories.

Chapter 7: Holiday Décor on Demand
"Deck the Halls in 30 Minutes or Less"

The holidays are here, and you're short on time to transform your space into a festive wonderland. Whether unexpected guests are arriving, or you just realized your home could use a little extra holiday cheer, this chapter provides quick, simple, and budget-friendly decorating ideas. Using items you already have—or can source quickly—you'll learn how to maximize the holiday spirit with minimal effort.

The 30-Minute Decorating Strategy

Before diving into specific ideas, here's a quick strategy to make decorating efficient and stress-free:

1. **Focus on High-Impact Areas:** Concentrate on the spots guests are most likely to see, such as the living room, dining area, entryway, and windows.
2. **Use What You Have:** Look around your home for items that can be repurposed or reimagined into holiday décor.
3. **Set a Timer:** Allocate a few minutes to each area to ensure you stay on track.
4. **Embrace Imperfection:** Decorations don't need to be perfect; they just need to create a festive atmosphere.

Quick Decorating Ideas for Each Area
1. Living Room

- **Throw Blankets and Pillows:** Drape red, green, or plaid blankets over sofas and chairs. Add pillows with festive colors or patterns.
- **DIY Mantel Décor:** Use candles, pinecones, and greenery (real or faux) to decorate your mantel. If you don't have a fireplace, arrange these items on a coffee table or shelf.
- **Mini Christmas Tree:** If a full-sized tree isn't an option, place a small tabletop tree in a visible corner. Decorate it with ribbons, ornaments, or even strings of popcorn.

2. Dining Area

- **Festive Centerpiece:** Fill a bowl or vase with ornaments, pinecones, or fresh fruit like apples and oranges. Add a sprig of greenery or a few candles for a polished look.
- **Table Setting:** Use mismatched plates and glasses for a charming, rustic vibe. Tie napkins with ribbon or twine and add a sprig of rosemary or a candy cane as a festive touch.
- **Holiday Runner:** If you don't have a table runner, use a scarf or strip of wrapping paper to add color and pattern.

3. Entryway

- **Welcome Wreath:** If you don't have a wreath, make one by tying together branches, greenery, or even ribbon into a circular shape.
- **String Lights:** Drape lights around your doorframe or along the staircase. Battery-operated lights work well in areas without outlets.

- **Holiday Scents:** Place a bowl of potpourri or simmer a pot of water with cinnamon sticks, cloves, and orange slices to greet guests with a festive aroma.

4. Windows

- **Simple Garlands:** Drape greenery or tinsel along the tops of windows. Add bows or ornaments for extra flair.
- **Window Clings:** If you have holiday stickers or clings, apply them to create a cheerful display.
- **DIY Snowflakes:** Cut snowflakes from white paper and tape them to the windows for a wintery feel.

5. Kitchen

- **Countertop Décor:** Arrange a few festive mugs, jars of candy canes, or a plate of cookies on the counter.
- **Holiday Towels:** Swap out your regular dish towels for ones with holiday patterns or colors.
- **Mini Garland:** Hang a small garland or ribbon across your cabinets or shelves for a subtle touch.

Decorating with Everyday Items

When time and resources are limited, everyday household items can double as holiday décor:

- **Books:** Stack books with red, green, or gold covers into a "tree" shape or use them as risers for candles and ornaments.
- **Mason Jars:** Fill jars with fairy lights, candy, or small ornaments. Tie a ribbon around the top for a festive finish.
- **Blankets:** Use cozy blankets to create a warm, layered look on furniture or as tree skirts.
- **Twine and Ribbon:** Wrap twine or ribbon around candles, vases, or jars to add a rustic holiday touch.
- **Kitchen Staples:** Use cookie cutters, dried fruit, or spices like cinnamon sticks as part of your decorations.

Last-Minute DIY Projects
1. Ornament Garland

- **What You Need:** String, ribbon, or twine; leftover ornaments.
- **How to Make It:** Thread the ornaments onto the string, spacing them evenly. Hang the garland on the mantel, across a window, or along a staircase.

2. Festive Candles

- **What You Need:** Plain candles, cinnamon sticks, ribbon.
- **How to Make It:** Wrap cinnamon sticks around the base of the candle and secure with ribbon. Place on a plate with greenery or small ornaments.

3. Holiday Banner

- **What You Need:** Paper, markers, scissors, string.

- **How to Make It:** Cut triangles or rectangles from paper and write holiday messages like "Merry Christmas" or "Joy." String them together and hang in a prominent spot.

4. Pinecone Place Cards

- **What You Need:** Pinecones, paper, and a marker.
- **How to Make It:** Write guest names on small pieces of paper and wedge them between the pinecone scales. Use as place cards at the table.

Budget-Friendly Store Finds

If you need to purchase a few items quickly, look for these affordable options:

1. **Dollar Stores:** Stock up on ornaments, garlands, and festive napkins or plates.
2. **Thrift Stores:** Look for vintage holiday decorations, candles, or cozy blankets.
3. **Grocery Stores:** Grab fresh flowers, greenery, or pre-made holiday arrangements.
4. **Pharmacies:** Many drugstores carry seasonal décor like stockings, wreaths, and string lights.

Lighting: Instant Holiday Ambiance

Lighting can transform a space instantly. Here's how to create a festive glow:

- **String Lights:** Wrap them around banisters, drape them over curtains, or place them in jars for a magical effect.
- **Candles:** Use pillar candles, tea lights, or LED candles to add warmth and coziness.

- **Fairy Lights:** Battery-operated fairy lights are versatile and easy to place anywhere.

Setting the Mood with Scents and Sounds

Holiday ambiance isn't just visual. Engage the senses with festive scents and music:

- **Scents:** Simmer a pot of water with cinnamon sticks, cloves, and orange peels, or use holiday-scented candles like pine, cinnamon, or vanilla.
- **Sounds:** Play a holiday playlist or traditional carols to create a joyful atmosphere.

Conclusion: Festive Flair in a Flash

Holiday decorating doesn't need to take hours or cost a fortune. With a little creativity and resourcefulness, you can transform your home into a festive haven in just 30 minutes. Remember, it's the thought and effort that count, and sometimes the simplest touches create the most memorable holiday vibes. So grab a few items, set a timer, and let the holiday spirit shine!

Chapter 8: Tech Troubles
"Fixing Festive Failures"

The holidays are a time for connection—whether through video calls with distant family, streaming your favorite holiday movies, or relying on online shopping to deliver those last-minute gifts. But when technology fails, the festive spirit can quickly turn into frustration. This chapter provides practical solutions for common tech issues, ensuring your gadgets, networks, and online services keep running smoothly throughout the holiday season.

1. Wi-Fi Outages: Staying Connected

A Wi-Fi outage can grind holiday plans to a halt, disrupting video calls, online shopping, and even smart home decorations. Here's how to troubleshoot and resolve connectivity issues quickly:

Quick Fixes

- **Restart Your Router:** Unplug the router for 30 seconds and then plug it back in. Allow it to reboot fully before testing the connection.
- **Check Connections:** Ensure all cables are securely connected and that there's no visible damage.
- **Positioning Matters:** Place your router in a central, elevated location away from walls or large metal objects to improve signal strength.
- **Switch to Ethernet:** If possible, use an Ethernet cable for critical tasks like streaming or video calls.

Advanced Solutions

- **Reset Network Settings:** On your device, forget the network and reconnect by entering the password again.
- **Use a Mobile Hotspot:** Temporarily switch to your phone's hotspot if the Wi-Fi issue persists.
- **Check for Outages:** Visit your internet service provider's website or call their support line to see if there's a known issue in your area.

Prevention Tips

- Invest in a Wi-Fi range extender or mesh system to eliminate dead zones.
- Schedule bandwidth-heavy activities, like downloading large files, during off-peak hours to avoid congestion.

2. Gadget Malfunctions: Troubleshooting Devices

From smart speakers to TVs and laptops, gadgets are the backbone of modern holiday fun. When they act up, here's how to get them back on track:

Common Issues and Fixes

- **Unresponsive Devices:**
  - Restart the device by turning it off, unplugging it, and waiting 30 seconds before powering it back on.
  - Check for software updates that might fix bugs or improve performance.
- **Overheating:**
  - Avoid placing devices near heat sources like fireplaces.
  - Give gadgets a break if they've been in continuous use for several hours.
- **Frozen Screens:**

- Perform a hard reset by holding down the power button for 10–15 seconds.
- For computers, use Ctrl + Alt + Delete (Windows) or Command + Option + Escape (Mac) to force close unresponsive apps.

Smart Home Devices

- **Alexa/Google Home Not Responding:**
  - Ensure they're connected to the correct Wi-Fi network.
  - Reboot the device and reconfigure it in the app if needed.
- **Smart Plugs and Lights Not Working:**
  - Confirm they're connected to the same network as your phone or smart hub.
  - Check the app for firmware updates or troubleshoot connectivity issues.

3. Online Shopping Glitches: Saving Your Holiday Orders

Last-minute shopping is stressful enough without website crashes or payment errors. Here's how to resolve common online shopping issues:

Failed Transactions

- **Double-Check Payment Info:** Ensure your card details, billing address, and CVV code are entered correctly.
- **Try a Different Browser:** Some sites work better in specific browsers (e.g., Chrome vs. Safari).
- **Clear Cache and Cookies:** Go to your browser settings and clear cached data to fix glitches.

Website Crashes

- **Refresh or Wait:** Reload the page after a few minutes. Many retailers update their servers quickly during peak times.
- **Use the Mobile App:** Apps are often more stable than websites during high traffic.
- **Switch to a Competitor:** If time is critical, check other retailers for the same or similar items.

Tracking Delays

- **Use Delivery Apps:** Services like Shop and Route consolidate tracking info across multiple retailers, providing updates in one place.
- **Contact Customer Support:** Call or chat with the retailer for the latest status on your order.

4. Streaming Issues: Keeping the Holiday Spirit Alive

Buffering or unresponsive streaming services can ruin a cozy holiday movie night. Try these fixes:

Video Buffering

- **Lower Video Quality:** Reduce the resolution (e.g., from 4K to 1080p) to minimize buffering.
- **Pause Downloads:** Stop any ongoing downloads or updates on other devices using the same network.
- **Restart Devices:** Reboot your streaming device and router to refresh the connection.

App Crashes

- **Update the App:** Check for the latest version in your device's app store.

- **Reinstall:** Uninstall and reinstall the app to clear any corrupted data.
- **Switch Devices:** Try using another device to access the streaming service.

Account Issues

- **Too Many Users Logged In:** Check your account settings and log out of devices no longer in use.
- **Subscription Problems:** Ensure your subscription is active and payments are up-to-date.

5. Tech Hygiene: Avoiding Overloads

With multiple devices in use during the holidays, tech overload is common. Prevent slowdowns and crashes by:

- **Closing Unused Apps:** Free up memory by closing apps and browser tabs not in use.
- **Rebooting Regularly:** Restart devices periodically to clear temporary files and improve performance.
- **Using Surge Protectors:** Protect electronics from power surges caused by holiday lighting or storms.

6. Data Backup and Recovery

Lost files or deleted photos can feel devastating, especially during the holidays. Here's how to safeguard your memories:

Backup Solutions

- **Cloud Storage:** Use services like Google Drive, iCloud, or Dropbox to back up important files and photos.
- **External Drives:** Save critical files to an external hard drive for offline access.

Recovery Tips

- **Accidentally Deleted Files:** Check the Recycle Bin (Windows) or Trash (Mac).
- **Photo Recovery:** Many smartphones have a "Recently Deleted" album where you can restore images within 30 days.
- **Use Recovery Software:** Tools like Disk Drill or Recuva can help recover lost files.

7. Staying Cyber-Safe During the Holidays

Holiday scams and phishing attacks peak during this time. Protect yourself with these tips:

- **Secure Wi-Fi:** Avoid shopping or banking over public Wi-Fi unless using a VPN.
- **Verify Emails:** Look out for typos, suspicious links, or requests for sensitive information in emails.
- **Use Strong Passwords:** Create unique passwords for online accounts and enable two-factor authentication wherever possible.

Conclusion: Mastering Holiday Tech

Tech troubles don't have to ruin your holiday festivities. With a proactive mindset and these quick fixes, you can keep your gadgets, networks, and online services running smoothly. Whether it's resolving a Wi-Fi outage, fixing an unresponsive gadget, or saving a failed online order, staying calm and resourceful will help you overcome any tech challenge and ensure your holiday season is merry and bright.

Chapter 9: Kids' Christmas Chaos
"Keeping Little Ones Happy and Entertained"

The holiday season is a magical time for children, but for parents juggling last-minute emergencies or hosting duties, keeping little ones entertained can feel like a full-time job. This chapter provides practical solutions to manage kids' boundless energy and excitement during the holidays, with a focus on engaging activities, simple crafts, and DIY gift ideas that not only keep them busy but also enhance their holiday experience.

1. Setting Up a Holiday Activity Zone

Create a dedicated space where kids can play, craft, and have fun independently while you handle other tasks.

Essentials for an Activity Zone

- **Craft Supplies:** Include items like crayons, markers, paper, scissors, glue, and glitter.
- **DIY Kits:** Assemble kits with pre-packaged materials for easy crafts (e.g., ornament decorating, card-making).
- **Books and Coloring Pages:** Choose holiday-themed coloring books and storybooks to keep the festive spirit alive.
- **Puzzles and Games:** Provide simple puzzles, board games, or card games suitable for their age.
- **Snack Station:** Set up a small table with healthy snacks and water to minimize interruptions.

Organizing the Space

- Use baskets or bins to separate different activities.
- Add a festive touch with string lights or a small table-top tree.
- Place a timer or clock nearby to give kids a sense of structure.

2. Easy Crafts to Keep Kids Engaged

Crafts are a fantastic way to channel kids' creativity while keeping them occupied. Here are some quick, mess-free ideas:

1. DIY Ornaments

- **Materials:** Popsicle sticks, glue, markers, ribbons, glitter, and sequins.
- **Instructions:**
    - Create snowflakes by gluing popsicle sticks into an X or star shape.
    - Decorate with paint, glitter, or stickers.
    - Tie a ribbon at the top for hanging.

2. Handprint Christmas Cards

- **Materials:** Cardstock, washable paint, markers.
- **Instructions:**
    - Have kids dip their hands in paint and press them onto the cardstock.
    - Turn the handprints into reindeer, Christmas trees, or Santa hats with markers.
    - Write holiday messages inside.

3. Pinecone Decorations

- **Materials:** Pinecones, white paint, glue, glitter, and small ribbons.

- **Instructions:**
  - Paint the tips of pinecones white for a snowy effect.
  - Add glitter and tie ribbons around the top.
  - Use as tree ornaments or table decorations.

4. Paper Snowflakes

- **Materials:** White paper, scissors.
- **Instructions:**
  - Fold paper into quarters or eighths.
  - Cut shapes along the edges.
  - Unfold to reveal intricate snowflake designs.

5. Festive Jars

- **Materials:** Mason jars, battery-operated fairy lights, ornaments, ribbons.
- **Instructions:**
  - Fill jars with fairy lights and small ornaments.
  - Tie a ribbon around the rim for a festive touch.

3. DIY Gifts Kids Can Make

Involving kids in making gifts not only keeps them entertained but also teaches them the joy of giving.

1. Cookie Mix in a Jar

- **Materials:** Mason jars, dry cookie ingredients (flour, sugar, chocolate chips), ribbon, and a recipe tag.
- **Instructions:**
  - Layer the dry ingredients in the jar.
  - Write or print the baking instructions on a tag.
  - Decorate the jar with ribbon and stickers.

2. Personalized Mugs

- **Materials:** Plain ceramic mugs, oil-based paint markers.
- **Instructions:**
    - Let kids draw designs or write messages on the mug.
    - Bake in the oven at 350°F for 30 minutes to set the design.

3. Salt Dough Ornaments

- **Materials:** Flour, salt, water, cookie cutters, paint.
- **Instructions:**
    - Mix 2 cups of flour, 1 cup of salt, and 1 cup of water to create dough.
    - Roll out and cut shapes with cookie cutters.
    - Bake at 200°F for 2 hours. Once cool, paint and add ribbon.

4. Beaded Bracelets or Keychains

- **Materials:** Beads, string, and keychain rings.
- **Instructions:**
    - String beads in festive colors or spell out the recipient's name.
    - Tie securely or attach to a keychain ring.

4. Engaging Holiday Games

Interactive games can burn off energy and keep kids entertained while you focus on other tasks.

1. Christmas Bingo

- **Materials:** Printable bingo cards with holiday images (snowman, tree, candy cane), markers or buttons.
- **Instructions:**

- ◦ Call out items for kids to mark off.
- ◦ The first to get a row, column, or diagonal wins.

2. Pin the Nose on Rudolph

- **Materials:** Poster of Rudolph, a red paper circle, blindfold.
- **Instructions:**
  - ◦ Blindfold kids and have them try to pin the nose on Rudolph.
  - ◦ Award small prizes for participation.

3. Holiday Scavenger Hunt

- **Materials:** List of holiday-themed items (e.g., candy cane, ornament, Santa hat).
- **Instructions:**
  - ◦ Hide items around the house and give kids the list.
  - ◦ Offer a prize for finding everything.

4. Snowball Toss

- **Materials:** White socks rolled into "snowballs," baskets or buckets.
- **Instructions:**
  - ◦ Set up targets and have kids toss the snowballs into them.
  - ◦ Award points for each successful toss.

5. Screen-Time Solutions

Sometimes, a bit of screen time is the easiest way to entertain kids while you manage holiday preparations. Here are some festive and educational options:

Holiday Movies and Shows

- **Recommendations:**
    - *The Polar Express*
    - *Home Alone*
    - *A Charlie Brown Christmas*
    - *How the Grinch Stole Christmas*

Educational Apps

- **Suggestions:**
    - *Khan Academy Kids*: Educational games and activities.
    - *PBS Kids Games*: Holiday-themed games and puzzles.

Interactive Videos

- Platforms like YouTube offer kid-friendly holiday craft tutorials or storytime videos.

6. Mindful Activities for Quiet Moments

When the excitement gets overwhelming, encourage kids to unwind with calm, mindful activities:

- **Holiday-Themed Coloring Pages:** Print free designs online for a relaxing art session.
- **Storytime:** Read classic holiday tales like *The Night Before Christmas* or *The Nutcracker.*
- **DIY Snow Globes:** Fill jars with water, glitter, and small holiday figurines.

7. Encouraging Kids to Help with Holiday Prep

Turn your to-do list into an opportunity for family bonding by involving kids in age-appropriate tasks:

- **Gift Wrapping:** Let kids decorate packages with stickers or help tape paper.
- **Baking:** Assign simple tasks like mixing batter, cutting cookie shapes, or decorating.
- **Setting the Table:** Kids can fold napkins, arrange silverware, or add place cards.
- **Tidying Up:** Turn cleanup into a game by timing how fast they can pick up toys or clear a room.

Conclusion: Managing Kids' Chaos with Creativity

The holidays are filled with magic and excitement for children, but managing their energy while juggling other responsibilities can feel overwhelming. By creating engaging activities, involving them in crafts or DIY gifts, and providing structured play, you can keep little ones entertained and happy. With these strategies, you'll not only manage the chaos but create meaningful memories they'll cherish for years to come.

Chapter 10: Financial Fixes
"Budget-Friendly Solutions for Last-Minute Needs"

The holidays are a time for joy and generosity, but last-minute expenses can quickly stretch your budget to its limits. Whether it's an unexpected gift exchange, a forgotten stocking, or higher-than-expected grocery bills, the season's surprises can leave you scrambling. This chapter offers practical, creative, and budget-friendly solutions to handle unexpected holiday expenses without breaking the bank.

1. Prioritizing Spending: The Holiday Necessities

The first step to managing holiday expenses is deciding what truly matters. Prioritize your spending to focus on what brings the most joy and impact.

Steps to Prioritize Your Holiday Budget

1. **Identify Essentials:** Focus on must-haves like gifts for immediate family, basic holiday meals, and essential decorations.
2. **Trim Non-Essentials:** Skip or scale back on extras, such as elaborate party supplies or excessive stocking stuffers.
3. **Set Spending Limits:** Allocate a specific amount for each category (gifts, food, travel) and stick to it.
4. **Track Your Spending:** Use a budgeting app like Mint or a simple spreadsheet to monitor expenses.

2. Creative Ways to Stretch Your Budget

When funds are tight, creativity can make every dollar go further.

1. DIY Gifts and Decorations

- **Homemade Gifts:** Create personalized presents, such as baked goods, photo albums, or handcrafted items.

- **DIY Decorations:** Use household items like mason jars, paper, and natural elements (pinecones, branches) to make festive décor.
- **Repurpose Old Items:** Turn last year's wrapping paper or old gift bags into this year's decorations or tags.

2. Utilize Rewards and Points

- **Credit Card Rewards:** Redeem points or cashback rewards for gift cards or holiday purchases.
- **Loyalty Programs:** Check if you've accumulated points with stores you frequent. Many retailers offer holiday bonuses for loyalty members.
- **Gift Cards:** Use any unused gift cards from previous holidays to offset costs.

3. Bulk Buying and Sharing Costs

- **Buy in Bulk:** Purchase larger quantities of items like food, wrapping paper, or generic gifts to save per unit.
- **Cost Sharing:** Split the cost of larger gifts or holiday meals with family or friends.

3. Saving Money on Last-Minute Gifts

Last-minute shopping doesn't have to mean overspending. Here are strategies for affordable and thoughtful gift-giving:

1. Affordable Gift Options

- **Regift Thoughtfully:** Pass along unused or lightly used items that you know someone else will love.
- **Create Experience Vouchers:** Write "coupons" for experiences like a movie night, homemade dinner, or a day of babysitting.
- **Shop Discount Stores:** Check stores like Dollar Tree, Five Below, or local thrift shops for unique and budget-friendly gifts.

- **Group Gifts:** Collaborate with others to give a single, meaningful gift, like a family photo book or a group outing.

2. Online Deals

- **Last-Minute Sales:** Many retailers offer discounts on gift cards or digital downloads (e-books, subscriptions) close to Christmas.
- **Flash Sales and Coupons:** Check sites like RetailMeNot, Honey, or Rakuten for discount codes.
- **Digital Gifts:** Send digital gift cards, streaming subscriptions, or memberships that require no shipping.

4. Reducing Holiday Food Costs

Holiday meals can be one of the biggest expenses. Here's how to enjoy a festive feast without overspending:

1. Budget-Friendly Menu Planning

- **Stick to Staples:** Focus on traditional dishes that use affordable, readily available ingredients like potatoes, carrots, and bread.
- **Limit Variety:** Instead of preparing multiple side dishes, stick to a few favorites.
- **Plan for Leftovers:** Choose dishes that can be repurposed into meals for the following days.

2. Affordable Ingredient Alternatives

- **Swap Expensive Proteins:** Replace turkey or ham with more affordable options like chicken, pork loin, or a vegetarian main dish.
- **Use Store Brands:** Opt for generic versions of baking supplies, canned goods, and spices to save money.
- **Buy Frozen or Canned Produce:** These are often cheaper and just as nutritious as fresh options.

3. Potluck-Style Meals

- **Share the Load:** Ask guests to bring a dish or dessert to contribute to the meal.
- **Theme the Menu:** Create a theme like "Comfort Foods" or "Holiday Classics" to make contributions easier to plan.

5. Budget-Friendly Holiday Activities

Creating memories doesn't have to come with a hefty price tag. Focus on low-cost or free activities that bring joy to the season.

Free or Low-Cost Holiday Activities

- **Movie Marathon:** Stream holiday classics at home with popcorn and hot cocoa.
- **DIY Craft Night:** Create decorations, cards, or ornaments together as a family.
- **Neighborhood Lights Tour:** Drive or walk around your neighborhood to admire holiday light displays.
- **Bake Together:** Spend an afternoon baking cookies or assembling gingerbread houses.

Community Events

- **Local Parades or Festivals:** Many towns host free holiday events like tree lightings or caroling.
- **Library Activities:** Check your local library for free holiday storytimes or craft workshops.
- **Charity Work:** Volunteering as a family at a food bank or shelter can be a meaningful way to spend the season.

6. Managing Debt and Financial Stress

The holidays can be a strain on your finances, but careful planning and smart choices can help you avoid debt and stress.

Debt-Free Strategies

- **Use Cash Only:** Withdraw your holiday budget in cash to prevent overspending.
- **Avoid Credit Card Traps:** Pay with debit or cash instead of racking up interest on credit card balances.
- **Opt for Layaway Plans:** Some stores offer layaway options that let you pay in installments without interest.

Handling Financial Stress

- **Communicate with Family:** Be honest about your budget and suggest cost-saving alternatives like Secret Santa or homemade gifts.
- **Focus on Gratitude:** Shift the focus from material gifts to meaningful experiences and connections.
- **Plan for Next Year:** Start saving for next year's holidays by setting aside a small amount each month.

7. Leveraging Technology to Save Money

Use digital tools to find savings and manage your holiday spending:

1. Price Comparison Apps

- **Apps to Try:** Use tools like ShopSavvy or PriceGrabber to compare prices across multiple retailers.

2. Cashback Apps

- **Get Money Back:** Apps like Rakuten or Ibotta offer cashback on holiday purchases.

3. Budgeting Tools

- **Track Spending:** Apps like Mint or YNAB (You Need A Budget) can help you monitor your holiday expenses in real time.

8. Frugal Alternatives to Holiday Traditions

You don't have to abandon beloved holiday traditions—just modify them to fit your budget:

1. Gift-Giving

- **Secret Santa:** Limit the number of gifts exchanged by organizing a Secret Santa or White Elephant exchange.
- **Handmade Gifts:** Focus on heartfelt, homemade items instead of store-bought ones.

2. Decorating

- **Minimalist Decor:** Use natural elements like pine branches, oranges, and candles for an affordable, rustic aesthetic.
- **Repurpose Old Decorations:** Refresh last year's décor by adding paint, glitter, or new arrangements.

3. Meals

- **Breakfast Potluck:** Simplify Christmas morning with a casual potluck breakfast.
- **Soup and Bread Dinner:** Swap the traditional feast for a cozy, affordable meal like homemade soup and bread.

Conclusion: A Festive Season Without Financial Strain

The holidays don't have to be financially overwhelming. With thoughtful planning, creative alternatives, and smart spending strategies, you can navigate last-minute expenses while staying within your budget. Remember, the true spirit of the season isn't about how much you spend—it's about the joy, love, and connections you share. By focusing on what matters most, you'll create a meaningful and memorable holiday season without breaking the bank.

Chapter 11: The Unexpected Guest Dilemma
"Welcoming Surprise Visitors with Ease"

Few holiday moments bring more pressure than the sudden arrival of unexpected guests. Whether it's a neighbor dropping by, relatives making an impromptu visit, or friends surprising you, the key to navigating these situations is preparation, resourcefulness, and a dash of creativity. This chapter offers practical advice on accommodating surprise visitors, including last-minute meal prep, thoughtful gift ideas, and quick cleaning hacks to create a warm and inviting atmosphere without breaking a sweat.

1. Embracing a Welcoming Mindset

The most important ingredient for hosting unexpected guests is your attitude. A calm, gracious demeanor puts everyone at ease. Remember, your visitors aren't expecting perfection—they're there for connection and holiday cheer.

Tips for Staying Calm

- **Take a Deep Breath:** Prioritize making guests feel welcome rather than stressing about every detail.
- **Focus on What Matters:** Guests will remember your warmth and hospitality, not whether every corner of the house is spotless.
- **Prepare Mentally for the Unexpected:** Accept that surprises happen, especially during the holidays, and treat them as opportunities for spontaneous joy.

2. Quick Cleaning Hacks for an Inviting Home

Even if your home isn't guest-ready, a few strategic cleaning moves can make it feel tidy and welcoming in minutes.

Focus on High-Impact Areas

- **Living Room:** Fluff pillows, fold blankets, and clear clutter from tables.
- **Bathroom:** Wipe down the sink, replace hand towels, and ensure soap and toilet paper are stocked.
- **Entryway:** Sweep the floor, clear shoes, and hang coats neatly.

Speed Cleaning Tips

- **Basket Trick:** Toss clutter into a basket or box and hide it in a closet temporarily.
- **All-Purpose Cleaner:** Keep a bottle of multi-surface cleaner and microfiber cloth handy for quick wipe-downs.
- **Vacuum Traffic Areas:** Focus on high-traffic zones rather than the whole house.
- **Use Candles or Air Fresheners:** A pleasant scent creates an immediate sense of cleanliness and coziness.

Lighting for Ambiance

- Dim harsh overhead lights and rely on lamps, string lights, or candles to create a warm, inviting glow.

3. Last-Minute Meal Prep

When guests arrive unannounced, feeding them can feel daunting. Keep it simple and use pantry staples to create quick, crowd-pleasing meals or snacks.

Appetizer Ideas

- **Charcuterie Board:** Use whatever you have—cheese, crackers, nuts, dried fruit, and sliced meats. Arrange them on a cutting board for a polished presentation.
- **Chips and Dip:** Pair tortilla chips with salsa, guacamole, or even hummus. Yogurt mixed with ranch seasoning makes an easy dip substitute.
- **Vegetable Platter:** Slice carrots, cucumbers, and celery, and serve with a quick dip.

Easy Main Courses

- **Pasta Dish:** Toss cooked pasta with jarred marinara or alfredo sauce. Add shredded cheese or frozen veggies for extra flavor.
- **Soup and Sandwiches:** Heat canned soup and pair with grilled cheese or deli sandwiches.
- **One-Pot Rice Dish:** Sauté rice with frozen vegetables, soy sauce, and eggs for a quick stir-fry.

Dessert in Minutes

- **Hot Chocolate Bar:** Set out mugs, cocoa mix, milk or water, and toppings like marshmallows or whipped cream.
- **Fruit and Yogurt Parfaits:** Layer yogurt, fruit, and granola in glasses for a fast, healthy treat.

- **Store-Bought Cookies:** Warm cookies slightly in the oven to give them a homemade feel.

4. Thoughtful Last-Minute Gift Ideas

Unexpected guests don't mean you need to empty your wallet. These simple, thoughtful gifts can be put together quickly:

Grab-and-Go Options

- **Holiday Candles:** Keep a few unscented or festive candles on hand as versatile gifts.
- **Baked Goods:** Wrap cookies or brownies in cellophane and tie with a ribbon.
- **Potted Plants:** Small succulents or herbs make charming, low-maintenance gifts.

DIY Gifts

- **Custom Hot Cocoa Mix:** Combine cocoa powder, sugar, and a pinch of salt in a jar. Add mini marshmallows or a candy cane for decoration.
- **Personalized Ornaments:** Write their name or a short holiday message on plain ornaments with a paint pen.
- **Homemade Sachets:** Fill small fabric pouches with dried lavender, cinnamon sticks, or cloves for a fragrant gift.

Regifting Smartly

- **Unused Items:** Pass along new, unopened items (like wine, books, or candles) you've received but don't need.
- **Add a Personal Touch:** Include a handwritten note to make the gift feel special and intentional.

5. Engaging Guests with Holiday Activities

Keep surprise visitors entertained with simple, festive activities that require minimal setup.

Conversation Starters

- Share favorite holiday memories or traditions.
- Ask guests about their holiday plans or favorite seasonal treats.

Quick Group Activities

- **Christmas Karaoke:** Use YouTube or a karaoke app for a fun, impromptu sing-along.
- **Holiday Trivia:** Prepare a few trivia questions about holiday movies, songs, or traditions.
- **Card Games:** Simple games like Uno or Go Fish are easy to set up and enjoy with all ages.

For Kids:

- Set up a small craft station with crayons, paper, and stickers.
- Play a quick round of "Pin the Nose on Rudolph" or a holiday scavenger hunt.

6. Staying Stocked for Surprises

Being prepared for unexpected guests doesn't require an elaborate setup. Keep a few essentials on hand to make hosting easier:

Pantry Staples:

- Crackers, nuts, canned soup, pasta, jarred sauces, and coffee/tea.

Freezer Finds:

- Frozen appetizers like mini quiches or spring rolls.
- Frozen cookie dough or pre-made desserts.

Gift Drawer:

- Store a few generic gifts like candles, small bottles of wine, or holiday mugs.

Emergency Cleaning Kit:

- All-purpose cleaner, microfiber cloths, and air freshener.

Decor Essentials:

- Extra string lights, candles, or garlands to quickly refresh the space.

7. The Power of Presentation

Even simple touches can make your home feel special:

- **Set the Mood with Music:** Play soft holiday tunes in the background.
- **Offer a Warm Drink:** Greet guests with coffee, tea, or hot chocolate to make them feel welcome.

- **Use Seasonal Decor:** Arrange ornaments in a bowl, light candles, or drape a holiday-themed throw blanket over a chair.

8. Turning Surprises into Memories

Unexpected visits can be opportunities for spontaneous joy and meaningful moments. By embracing the surprise and focusing on connection, you'll create lasting holiday memories for both you and your guests.

Conclusion: Welcoming Guests with Confidence

Accommodating surprise visitors during the holidays doesn't have to be stressful. With quick cleaning hacks, easy meal ideas, and a stash of simple gifts, you can transform a potentially chaotic moment into an opportunity to showcase your warmth and hospitality. Remember, it's the thoughtfulness and effort you put into welcoming your guests that truly make them feel at home. So, take a deep breath, roll with the surprises, and let the holiday cheer shine through.

Chapter 12: Post-Holiday Recovery Plan
"Planning Ahead for Next Year"

As the holidays wind down and the new year approaches, it's the perfect time to reflect on the season's successes, challenges, and the lessons learned along the way. A well-thought-out recovery plan not only helps you decompress but also sets the stage for a smoother, more enjoyable holiday season next year. This chapter provides actionable strategies for organizing, planning, and avoiding future holiday crises.

1. Reflecting on the Season: What Worked and What Didn't

Start by taking stock of this year's holiday experience. Reflection helps identify areas for improvement while celebrating the moments that went well.

Questions to Ask Yourself

- What brought the most joy this season?
- Which activities or traditions felt stressful or unnecessary?
- Were there any last-minute crises that could have been avoided?
- Did you stick to your budget, or were there unexpected expenses?

How to Document Your Reflections

- **Holiday Journal:** Dedicate a notebook or digital document to jot down thoughts and lessons learned.
- **Photo Review:** Go through holiday photos to identify what worked well (e.g., decorations, meal setups, gift exchanges).
- **Family Feedback:** Ask loved ones what they enjoyed most and what they'd like to improve for next year.

2. Organizing Holiday Supplies

Avoid the frustration of digging through disorganized boxes next year by taking time to organize your holiday supplies now.

Step-by-Step Guide to Organizing

1. **Declutter:** Discard broken ornaments, outdated decorations, and items you didn't use.
2. **Categorize Supplies:** Group items by type (e.g., ornaments, lights, wrapping paper) and label containers clearly.
3. **Invest in Storage Solutions:**
    - Use sturdy bins with lids to protect items from dust and moisture.
    - For fragile items, consider padded containers or dividers.
    - Store string lights on reels or wrap them around cardboard to prevent tangles.
4. **Create an Inventory:** Keep a list of what you have to avoid over-buying next year. A simple spreadsheet or notes app works well.
5. **Designate a Storage Area:** Choose an accessible spot, such as a closet, attic, or garage, and keep holiday supplies together.

3. Budgeting for Next Year

Holiday expenses can add up quickly. Planning ahead financially ensures you're prepared without overspending.

Create a Holiday Savings Plan

- **Set a Budget:** Estimate next year's costs for gifts, meals, travel, and decorations.
- **Start Early:** Open a dedicated holiday savings account and contribute a small amount monthly.
- **Use Apps:** Apps like Mint or YNAB (You Need A Budget) can help track and allocate holiday funds.

Shop Smart All Year

- **Post-Holiday Sales:** Stock up on wrapping paper, cards, and decorations at deep discounts right after the holidays.
- **Gift Buying:** Purchase gifts throughout the year when you find great deals.
- **Reward Points:** Save credit card rewards or loyalty points to redeem for holiday shopping.

4. Planning Gifts in Advance

Avoid the last-minute rush by planning your gift list and shopping early.

Create a Master Gift List

- **Include Everyone:** List all recipients, including family, friends, teachers, and coworkers.
- **Brainstorm Ideas:** Note potential gifts for each person and update the list as ideas come to mind.

Start Shopping Early

- **Track Sales:** Use apps like Honey or CamelCamelCamel to monitor price drops.
- **Stockpile Small Gifts:** Keep a stash of generic items (candles, notebooks, gift cards) for unexpected gift exchanges.

Consider Homemade Gifts

- Plan DIY projects ahead of time, such as photo books, baked goods, or personalized crafts.

5. Early Decoration Preparation

Streamline next year's decorating process with these preparation tips:

Take Photos:

- Photograph your decorations this year for reference. It's a great way to replicate setups you loved or tweak areas you'd like to improve.

Repair and Replace:

- Fix broken ornaments, lights, or decorations before storing them. Make a note of any items you need to replace.

Pre-Label Storage Bins:

- Clearly label bins by room or area (e.g., "Living Room Tree," "Outdoor Lights") to make decorating faster and easier.

6. Simplifying Holiday Meals

Cooking for the holidays doesn't have to be stressful. Planning ahead can save time and effort next year.

Record Recipes and Feedback

- Keep a list of recipes that were hits and note any changes you'd make.
- Write down portions to avoid making too much or too little food.

Prepare Freezer-Friendly Dishes

- Identify meals or desserts you can prepare in advance and freeze for next year.

Stockpile Staples

- Buy non-perishable ingredients like spices, canned goods, or baking supplies during sales throughout the year.

7. Managing Time More Effectively

Time management is key to avoiding the last-minute rush. Use these strategies to plan next year's holidays more efficiently:

Create a Holiday Calendar

- Map out key dates for shopping, decorating, meal prep, and events.
- Start major tasks (e.g., gift shopping) at least a month earlier than you think necessary.

Delegate Tasks

- Assign responsibilities to family members, such as wrapping gifts, decorating, or setting the table.

Build in Buffer Time

- Plan for potential delays or interruptions by scheduling tasks earlier than needed.

8. Avoiding Common Holiday Stressors

Identify and address the stressors that caused the most trouble this year to ensure a smoother experience next time.

Examples and Solutions

- **Last-Minute Guests:** Keep extra snacks, gifts, and decorations on hand.
- **Shipping Delays:** Order gifts earlier and choose retailers with reliable delivery options.
- **Overcommitment:** Learn to say no to events or obligations that don't bring joy.

9. Incorporating Family Feedback

Involve your family in the planning process to create a holiday experience everyone enjoys.

Host a Family Debrief

- Discuss what everyone loved about this year and what could improve.
- Use their input to shape next year's activities and traditions.

Rotate Responsibilities

- Assign each family member a role, such as planning the menu, organizing decorations, or hosting a specific event.

10. Creating Traditions That Stick

The holidays are about more than logistics—they're about creating meaningful memories. Focus on traditions that matter most to your family.

Sustainable Traditions

- Choose traditions that are easy to repeat and don't require significant time or money.
- Examples: Baking cookies together, watching a holiday movie marathon, or volunteering as a family.

Conclusion: Building a Brighter Holiday Future

A little planning now can make next year's holidays less stressful and more joyful. By reflecting on lessons learned, organizing your supplies, and preparing early, you'll avoid many of the crises that arise during the holiday rush. Remember, the goal isn't perfection—it's creating a meaningful and enjoyable season for you and your loved ones. With these strategies in place, you're set to make next year's celebrations your best yet.

<u>Message from the Author:</u>

I hope you enjoyed this book, I love astrology and knew there was not a book such as this out on the shelf. I love metaphysical items as well. Please check out my other books:

-Life of Government Benefits

-My life of Hell

-My life with Hydrocephalus

-Red Sky

-World Domination:Woman's rule

-World Domination:Woman's Rule 2: The War

-Life and Banishment of Apophis: book 1

-The Kidney Friendly Diet

-The Ultimate Hemp Cookbook

-Creating a Dispensary(legally)

-Cleanliness throughout life: the importance of showering from childhood to adulthood.

-Strong Roots: The Risks of Overcoddling children

-Hemp Horoscopes: Cosmic Insights and Earthly Healing

- Celestial Hemp Navigating the Zodiac: Through the Green Cosmos

-Astrological Hemp: Aligning The Stars with Earth's Ancient Herb

-The Astrological Guide to Hemp: Stars, Signs, and Sacred Leaves

-Green Growth: Innovative Marketing Strategies for your Hemp Products and Dispensary

-Cosmic Cannabis

-Astrological Munchies

-Henry The Hemp

-Zodiacal Roots: The Astrological Soul Of Hemp

- **Green Constellations: Intersection of Hemp and Zodiac**

-Hemp in The Houses: An astrological Adventure Through The Cannabis Galaxy

-Galactic Ganja Guide

Heavenly Hemp

Zodiac Leaves

Doctor Who Astrology

Cannastrology

Stellar Satvias and Cosmic Indicas

Celestial Cannabis: A Zodiac Journey

AstroHerbology: The Sky and The Soil: Volume 1

AstroHerbology:Celestial Cannabis:Volume 2

Cosmic Cannabis Cultivation

The Starry Guide to Herbal Harmony: Volume 1

The Starry Guide to Herbal Harmony: Cannabis Universe: Volume 2

Yugioh Astrology: Astrological Guide to Deck, Duels and more

Nightmare Mansion: Echoes of The Abyss

Nightmare Mansion 2: Legacy of Shadows

Nightmare Mansion 3: Shadows of the Forgotten

Nightmare Mansion 4: Echoes of the Damned

The Life and Banishment of Apophis: Book 2

Nightmare Mansion: Halls of Despair

Healing with Herb: Cannabis and Hydrocephalus

Planetary Pot: Aligning with Astrological Herbs: Volume 1

Fast Track to Freedom: 30 Days to Financial Independence Using AI, Assets, and Agile Hustles

Cosmic Hemp Pathways

How to Become Financially Free in 30 Days: 10,000 Paths to Prosperity

Zodiacal Herbage: Astrological Insights: Volume 1

Nightmare Mansion: Whispers in the Walls

The Daleks Invade Atlantis

Henry the hemp and Hydrocephalus

10X The Kidney Friendly Diet

Cannabis Universe: Adult coloring book

Hemp Astrology: The Healing Power of the Stars

Zodiacal Herbage: Astrological Insights: Cannabis Universe: Volume 2

<u>Planetary Pot: Aligning with Astrological Herbs: Cannabis Universes: Volume 2</u>

Doctor Who Meets the Replicators and SG-1: The Ultimate Battle for Survival

Nightmare Mansion: Curse of the Blood Moon

<u>The Celestial Stoner: A Guide to the Zodiac</u>

Cosmic Pleasures: Sex Toy Astrology for Every Sign

Hydrocephalus Astrology: Navigating the Stars and Healing Waters

Lapis and the Mischievous Chocolate Bar

Celestial Positions: Sexual Astrology for Every Sign

Apophis's Shadow Work Journal: **:** A Journey of Self-Discovery and Healing

Kinky Cosmos: Sexual Kink Astrology for Every Sign

Digital Cosmos: The Astrological Digimon Compendium

Stellar Seeds: The Cosmic Guide to Growing with Astrology

Apophis's Daily Gratitude Journal

Cat Astrology: Feline Mysteries of the Cosmos

The Cosmic Kama Sutra: An Astrological Guide to Sexual Positions

Unleash Your Potential: A Guided Journal Powered by AI Insights

Whispers of the Enchanted Grove

Cosmic Pleasures: An Astrological Guide to Sexual Kinks

369, 12 Manifestation Journal

Whisper of the nocturne journal(blank journal for writing or drawing)

The Boogey Book

Locked In Reflection: A Chastity Journey Through Locktober

Generating Wealth Quickly:

How to Generate $100,000 in 24 Hours

Star Magic: Harness the Power of the Universe

The Flatulence Chronicles: A Fart Journal for Self-Discovery

The Doctor and The Death Moth

Seize the Day: A Personal Seizure Tracking Journal

The Ultimate Boogeyman Safari: A Journey into the Boogie World and Beyond

Whispers of Samhain: 1,000 Spells of Love, Luck, and Lunar Magic: Samhain Spell Book

Apophis's guides:

Witch's Spellbook Crafting Guide for Halloween

<u>Frost & Flame: The Enchanted Yule Grimoire of 1000 Winter Spells</u>

<u>The Ultimate Boogey Goo Guide & Spooky Activities for Halloween Fun</u>

Harmony of the Scales: A Libra's Spellcraft for Balance and Beauty

The Enchanted Advent: 36 Days of Christmas Wonders

Nightmare Mansion: The Labyrinth of Screams

Harvest of Enchantment: 1,000 Spells of Gratitude, Love, and Fortune for Thanksgiving

The Boogey Chronicles: A Journal of Nightly Encounters and Shadowy Secrets

The 12 Days of Financial Freedom: A Step-by-Step Christmas Countdown to Transform Your Finances

Sigil of the Eternal Spiral Blank Journal

A Christmas Feast: Timeless Recipes for Every Meal

Holiday Stress-Free Solutions: A Survival Guide to Thriving During the Festive Season

Yu-Gi-Oh! Holiday Gifting Mastery: The Ultimate Guide for Fans and Newcomers Alike

Holiday Harmony: A Hydrocephalus Survival Guide for the Festive Season

Celestial Craft: The Witch's Almanac for 2025 – A Cosmic Guide to Manifestations, Moons, and Mystical Events

Doctor Who: The Toymaker's Winter Wonderland

Tulsa King Unveiled: A Thrilling Guide to Stallone's Mafia Masterpiece

Pendulum Craft: A Complete Guide to Crafting and Using Personalized Divination Tools

Nightmare Mansion: Santa's Eternal Eve

Starlight Noel: A Cosmic Journey through Christmas Mysteries

The Dark Architect: Unlocking the Blueprint of Existence

Surviving the Embrace: The Ultimate Guide to Encounters with The Hugging Molly

The Enchanted Codex: Secrets of the Craft for Witches, Wiccans, and Pagans

Harvest of Gratitude: A Complete Thanksgiving Guide

Yuletide Essentials: A Complete Guide to an Authentic and Magical Christmas

Celestial Smokes: A Cosmic Guide to Cigars and Astrology

Living in Balance: A Comprehensive Survival Guide to Thriving with Diabetes Insipidus

Cosmic Symbiosis: The Venom Zodiac Chronicles

The Cursed Paw of Ambition

Cosmic Symbiosis: The Astrological Venom Journal

Celestial Wonders Unfold: A Stargazer's Guide to the Cosmos (2024-2029)

The Ultimate Black Friday Prepper's Guide: Mastering Shopping Strategies and Savings

Cosmic Sales: The Astrological Guide to Black Friday Shopping
Legends of the Corn Mother and Other Harvest Myths
Whispers of the Harvest: The Corn Mother's Journal
The Evergreen Spellbook
The Doctor Meets the Boogeyman
The White Witch of Rose Hall's SpellBook
The Gingerbread Golem's Shadow: A Study in Sweet Darkness
The Gingerbread Golem Codex: An Academic Exploration of Sweet Myths
The Gingerbread Golem Grimoire: Sweet Magicks and Spells for the Festive Witch
The Curse of the Gingerbread Golem
10-minute Christmas Crafts for kids

If you want solar for your home go here: https://www.harborso-lar.live/apophisenterprises/

Get Some Tarot cards: https://www.makeplayingcards.com/sell/apophis-occult-shop

Get some shirts: https://www.bonfire.com/store/apophis-shirt-emporium/

Instagrams:
@apophis_enterprises,
@apophisbookemporium,
@apophisscardshop
Twitter: @apophisenterpr1
 Tiktok:@apophisenterprise
Youtube: @sg1fan23477, @FiresideRetreatKingdom
Hive: @sg1fan23477
CheeLee: @SG1fan23477

Podcast: Apophis Chat Zone: https://open.spotify.com/show/ 5zXbrCLEV2xzCp8ybrfHsk?si=fb4d4fdbdce44dec

Newsletter: https://apophiss-newsletter-27c897.beehiiv.com/

Milton Keynes UK
Ingram Content Group UK Ltd.
UKHW022333041224
452010UK00019B/1136

9 798868 998409